Ichthyology

Book of COLORS

A Rainbow of Fish

AO PRESS

Jessica Lee Anderson

Paperback ISBN: 978-1-964078-50-2

To Ben, thanks for exploring nature with me when we were kids and even now as adults. I'm lucky to have you as my big brother! - JLA

Fish are often multi-colored, so have fun pointing out the variety of colors in addition to the featured colors! Photos are not to scale.

Photo credits, left to right, top to bottom: Front cover: Jonathan Hall (Rainbow parrotfish); Interior cover: johannes.k (Melanurus wrasse); Copyright page: johannes.k (Threadfin rainbow fish and dwarf neon rainbow fish); Dedication page: Pixs4u, johannes.k; p. 4: chollacholla, para827, nektofadeev@gmail.com; p. 5: Jeffry S.S, 1790462, hadot; p. 6: SONGSAKPANDET, LagunaticPhoto, Tom Brakefield; p. 7: missisya, Mirko_Rosenau, rschaubhut; p. 8: TongSur, richcarey, Mirko_Rosenau; p. 9: angipants, vojce, AG; p. 10: Vitalii Kalutskyi,_vojce, wrangel; p. 11: witte-art_de, RickRamos1973, FtLaudGirl; p. 12: Deepshine, Vpommeyrol, engabito; p. 13: Stéphane ROCHON, powerofforever, Motzing; p. 14: Filip Olcan, Mirko_Rosenau, Minakryn Ruslan; p. 15: Filip Olcan, vojce, 0846668891; p. 16: Natalie Ruffing, Katherine OBrien, sserg_dibrova; p. 17: vojce, Valentin Kundeus, BirdImages; p. 18: Jcomp, Laura Din, yelo34; p. 19: Miropa, Ryan Cake, Walter_Navarro; p. 20: Quality Stock Arts, kwanchaichaiudom, MATTHIASRABBIONE; p. 21: y-studio, Engin Akyurt, Ken Benitez; p. 22: Leonardo Lamas, LeoPatrizi, pclark2; p. 23: Serge Melesan, izanbar, gyro; p. 24: Global_Pics, PEDRE,_Kichigin ; p. 25: tunart, photographer3431, FishTales; p. 26: User10095428_393, Amy Kerk, Caden Van Cleave; p. 27: Jeffry Surianto, Dmitry Rukhlenko, Nichchima Anongjanya, showcake; p. 28: sergeyskleznev, shurub, CampPhoto; p. 29: Global_Pics,tunart, TatianaMironenko, Ayman Shalaby; 30: Magnus Larsson, Katherine OBrien, Yann-HUBERT; p. 31: Nigel Marsh, Jupiterimages, amriphoto, Rich Carey; p. 32: Irtish, vojce, Julialine; p. 33: slowmotiongli, mirecca, vojce, mirceax; p. 34: Michael Anderson; Back cover: southpict (Sohal tang)

This Book Belongs to:

_____

Ichthyology is the study of fish.

Betta

Guppy

Red

Betta

Swarthy parrotfish

Fish are animals that live in watery environments (aquatic).

Ember tetra

Red

Red arowana

Some species live in freshwater while others live in saltwater. Certain species can adapt to both types of water!

Red Sea coral grouper

Red platy

Orange

Goldfish

Lined seahorse

Fish are vertebrates, meaning they have backbones (vertebral columns).

Flame angelfish

Orange

Blood-red parrot cichlid

Gills are special organs that allow many species of fish to breathe underwater.

Galaxy rasbora

Common carp (koi)

Yellow

Betta

Shaggy frogfish

Certain types of fish have adapted to breathing air or have ways to survive without relying on gills.

Golden pleco

Yellow

Cow fish

There are many different kinds of fish found all around the world!

Yellow tang

Lemon tetra

9

Green

Stone fish

Green tiger barb

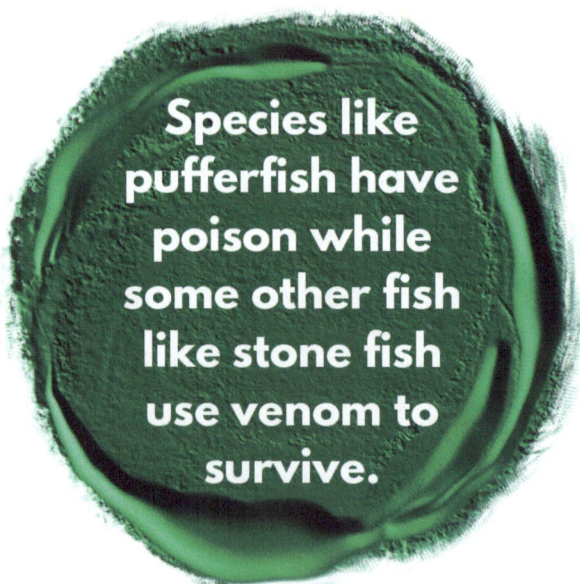

Species like pufferfish have poison while some other fish like stone fish use venom to survive.

Green-spotted puffer

Green

Leafy sea dragon

Many fish species blend into their environment (camouflage) to avoid predators or hunt prey.

Green moray eel

Dolphin fish (Mahi-mahi)

Blue

There are over 30,000 known fish species with more being discovered!

Swordfish

Blue shark

Blue tang

Blue

Electric blue damselfish

Blue discus

Humphead wrasse

Fish have been on Earth since ancient times— even before dinosaurs.

Purple

Purple tang

Emperor tetra

Fish live in a variety of habitats from coral reefs to ponds, rivers, and deep sea trenches.

Purple dottyback

Purple

Violet goby

Fins help fish balance, move, and steer while swimming in the water.

Striated wrasse

Betta

Pink

California sheephead

Emperor red snapper

Bright colors can scare off predators and serve as a source of communication within species, like attracting mates.

Sea goldie

Pink

Pink skunk clownfish

Bony fish species have protective scales and skeletons made of bone.

Pink tetra

Sockeye salmon

Black

Black sharkminnow

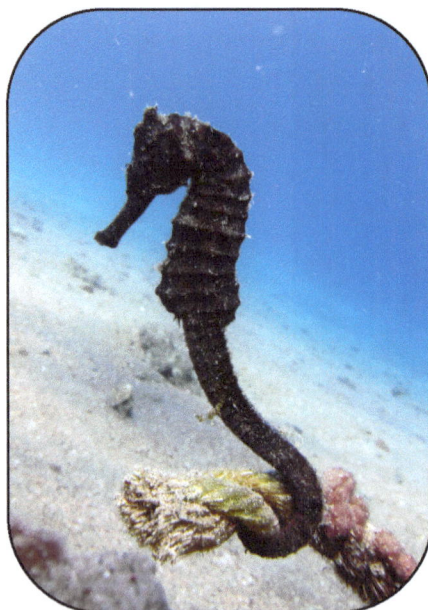
Black seahorse

Most fish dine on a variety of food sources like algae, insects, worms, crustaceans, and other fish.

Paddlefish

Black

Black sailfin molly

Sharks, stingrays, skates, and chimeras are types of fish with jaws and skeletons made of cartilage instead of bone.

Southern stingray

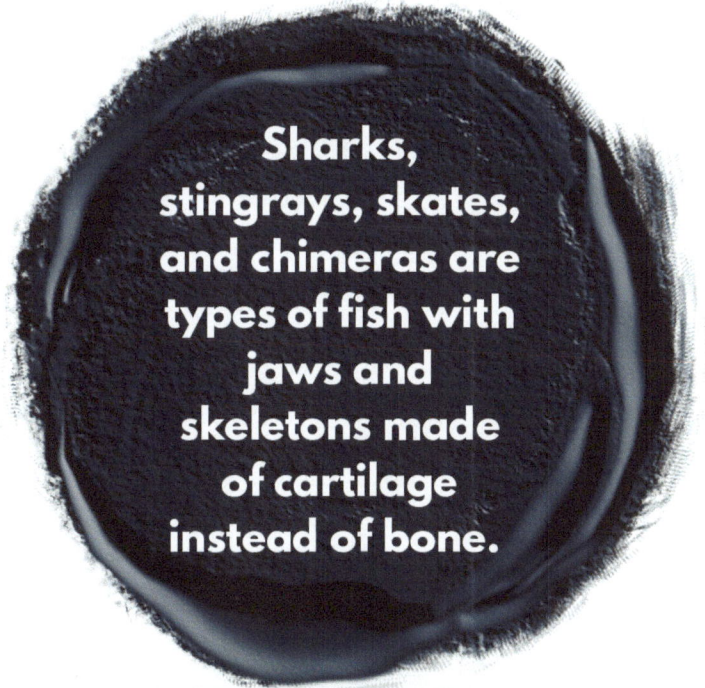

Black Moor goldfish

White

Butterfly carp (koi)

Bristlenosed pleco

Many fish species live together in groups, and some studies show they form social bonds.

Molly fish

White

White angelfish

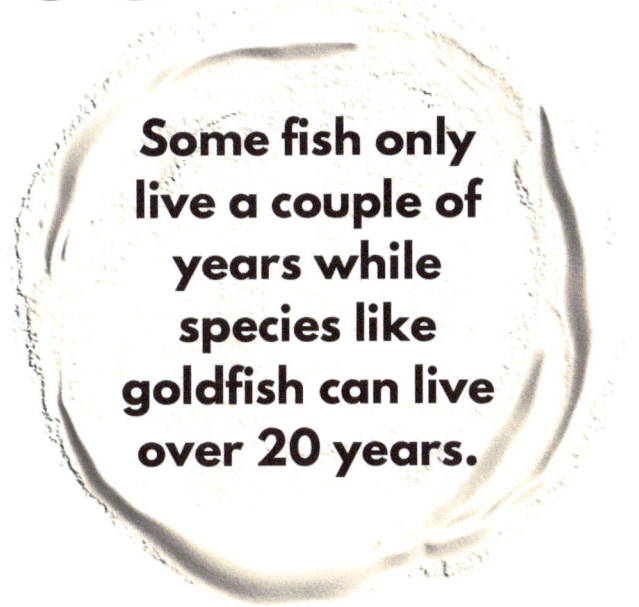

Some fish only live a couple of years while species like goldfish can live over 20 years.

Giant gourami

Betta

Gray

Whale shark

Ocean sunfish (Mola mola)

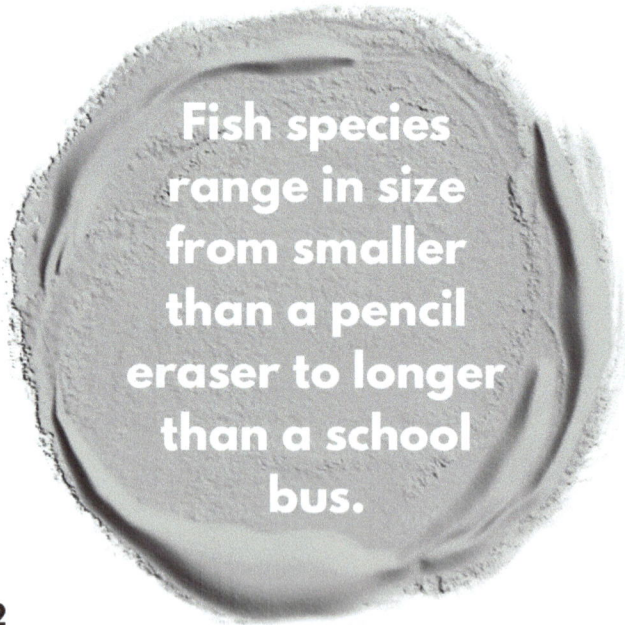

Fish species range in size from smaller than a pencil eraser to longer than a school bus.

Spot-fin porcupinefish

Gray

Hammerhead shark

A group of fish is called a school, and a group of sharks is called a shiver.

Sawfish

Wolf fish

Brown

Lemon shark (and remoras)

Sea lamprey

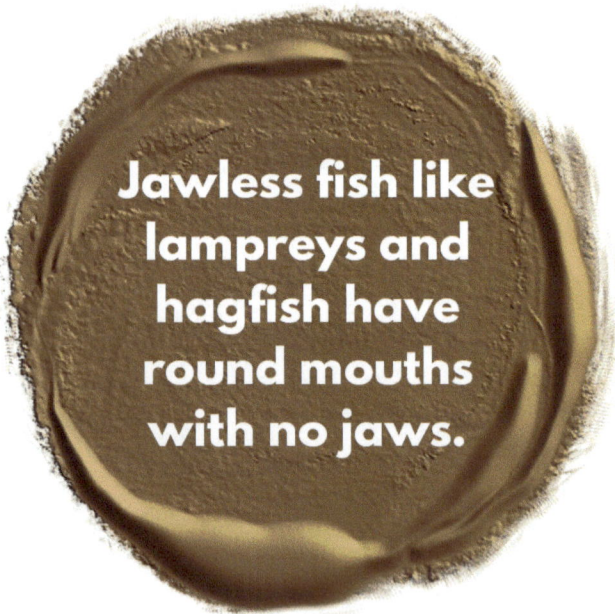

Jawless fish like lampreys and hagfish have round mouths with no jaws.

Scorpion fish

Brown

Alligator gar

Fish are essential for healthy ecosystems, and they are a source of food for many people and animals.

Brown trout

Thorny seahorse

COLOR Combinations

How are the colors of these fish species similar and different?

Rainbow cichlid

Rainbow trout

Rainbow darter

COLOR Combinations

Ribbon eel

Gardel eels

Pygmy seahorses

Flowerhorn cichlid

COLOR Combinations

What colors do these fish have in common? How are they different?

Discus

Emperor angelfish

Lagoon triggerfish

COLOR Combinations

Mandarin fish

Clown wrasse

Queen coris

Checkerboard wrasse

COLOR Combinations

What shapes and colors do you notice, and why do you think that is?

Lionfish

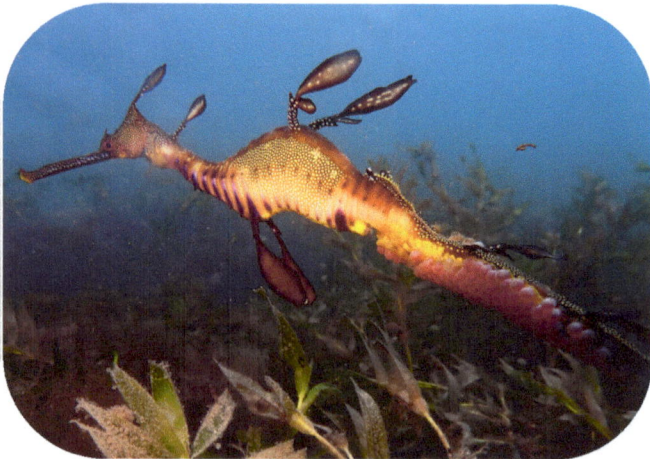

Weedy sea dragon

Stonefish

COLOR Combinations

Leopard shark

Peacock flounder

Blue-spotted stingray

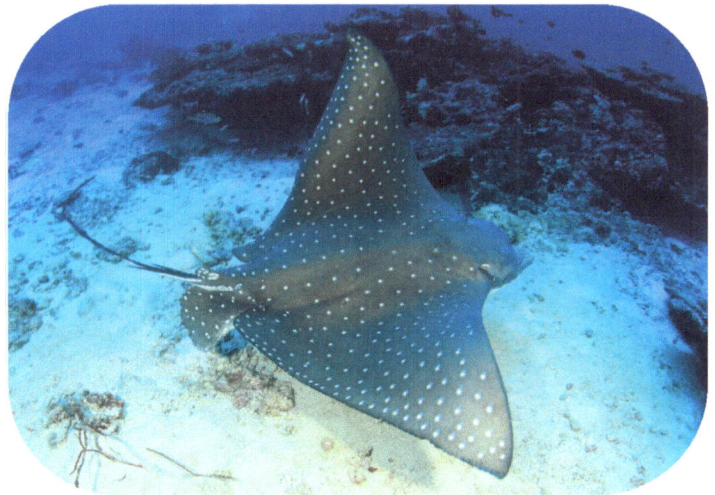
Spotted eagle ray

COLOR Combinations

Why do you think the colors, shapes, and features of a fish matter?

Schooling bannerfish

Banded pipefish

Clown fish

COLOR Combinations

Blue-headed wrasse

Red Sea steep-headed parrotfish

Mystery wrasse

German blue ram

Jessica Lee Anderson is an award-winning author of over 100 books for young readers to include the NAOMI NASH chapter book series. Jessica loves spending time in nature and exploring the outdoors with her husband, Michael, and their daughter, Ava! Jessica loves admiring fish, especially when snorkeling in Hawaii. You can learn more about Jessica by visiting www.jessicaleeanderson.com.

Check out these other books:

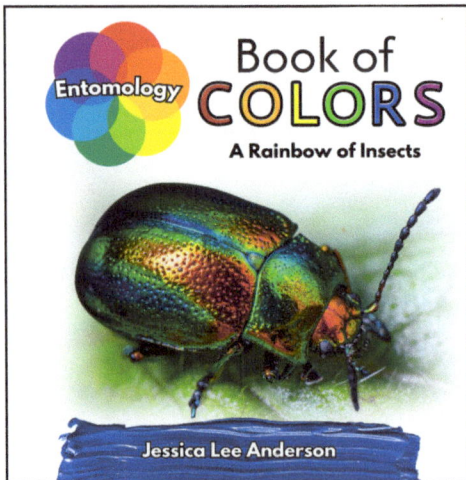

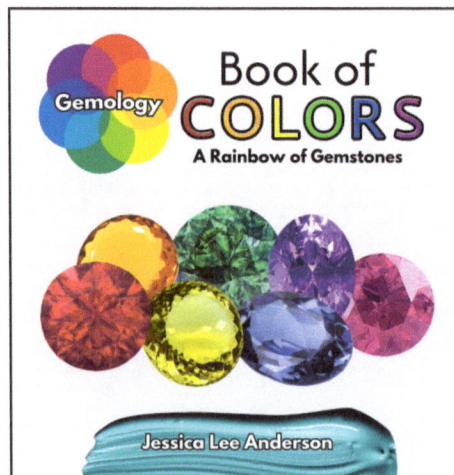

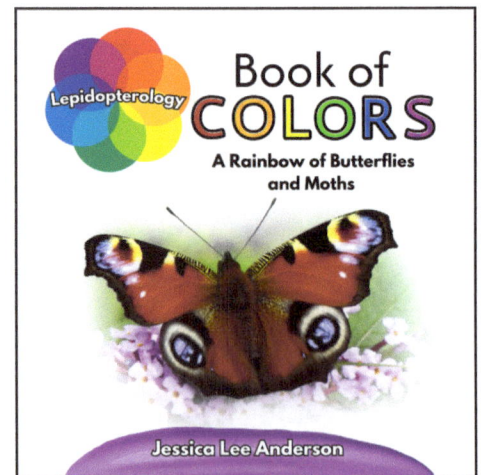

Entomology
Book of COLORS
A Rainbow of Insects
Jessica Lee Anderson

Gemology
Book of COLORS
A Rainbow of Gemstones
Jessica Lee Anderson

Lepidopterology
Book of COLORS
A Rainbow of Butterflies and Moths
Jessica Lee Anderson

www.ingramcontent.com/pod-product-compliance
Lightning Source LLC
Chambersburg PA
CBHW061144030426

42335CB00002B/102